The New Play Ethic at Work

by

Lynn Grasberg, CCO*
*Chief Comic Officer

Morningstar Communications LLC
Pagosa Springs, Colorado

www.bounceback.biz

Published by:
Morningstar Communications LLC
Post Office Box 5740, Pagosa Springs, CO 81147
970-731-9055
www.morningstar-media.com

Edited by:
Barbara McNichol

Cover and Ta-DAH Photo:
Stuart R. Royston

Cover Design:
Jonathan and Maurissa Morningstar,
Chrystos Minot

Illustrations:
Tod Puck Wills

ISBN 1-880047-95-0

Foreword

What a delight! What a joy! What an important gift ***Bounce Back!*** is for all those who need to recognize how vital humor is to succeed in business and in one's personal life. Laughter is a miracle drug and its therapeutic value cannot be overstated.

Lynn Grasberg, with extraordinary imagination and astonishing expertise, has provided all the necessary information to cope with sour-faced office managers, bad-tempered CEO's, stressed-out personnel directors as well as uptight colleagues who desperately need to lighten up.

Bounce Back! is an easy read with delightful illustrations to help make a point. It is great fun and best of all, offers the reader an opportunity to surf the waves of change, overcome downsizing and quickly recover from adversity.

Ms. Grasberg's practical and playful approach to using humor and developing a joyful spirit to improve teamwork and morale is whipped cream on the best strawberry shortcake of counsel you will ever devour.

LARRY WILDE
"America's Best-Selling Humorist"
Carmel, California

Publisher's Foreword

For 30 years, I worked too hard — often to the detriment of my health and well-being. I still work hard, but everything's changed now. Producing this book has challenged me to apply the "Play Ethic" rather than my former strategies of bullheadedness and self-denial.

What's made the difference? I'm learning to put play back into my work. I'm also learning to pay attention to what I really need as I go. Lynn Grasberg's practical and playful approach has shown me that "working hard" is not the only solution to getting the job done.

It's time for all of us to bring that playful spirit back to our jobs and all the other work we do at home and in our communities. It's time to find the humor in our daily lives and *really* Laugh Out Loud.

Lynn Grasberg is on a mission to help us do just that. This book is the fruit of her years on the playful path. Bite into it. Let the juice run down your chin. Take heart! Have fun.

Jonathan Morningstar
Publisher

Praise for *Bounce Back!*

I've worked in the high tech industry for years. We really need this book, especially with the volatility of our companies and resulting job insecurity of our employees. Thanks for making it so easy to read while containing so much immediately useful material. Your productively playful approach to work can really improve teamwork and morale.

Susana Escalante, Corporate Diversity Manager
Seagate Technology

My research in neuroscience highlights the effect of mood and attitude on physical health. *Bounce Back!* is a hands-on application of these ideas — a practical approach for elevating one's attitude without drugs. I enjoyed it personally and am delighted that this book is so effective at giving individuals permission to lighten up and improve their own health. This is psychoneuroimmunology in action!

Melissa K. Demetrikopoulos, Ph.D. ,
Director of Scientific Communications
Institute for Biomedical Philosophy

"Play as you go"management is a major improvement over the MBO garbage (Management by Objective) we've been doing for the past ten years! I was able to read *Bounce Back!* on the plane during a businesstrip. It's a quick, enjoyable read, filled with usable ideas and practical techniques for improving the work climate of any company. It has already helped me to lighten up and be more present. I highly recommend it.

Dennis Shaver, Executive Vice President
RapidPro Manufacturing

To handle the cascade of avalanching changes in your life, read, smile and have fun with Lynn's *Bounce Back!* ideas.

Mark Victor Hanson, Co-creator
#1 New York Times best-selling series,
Chicken Soup for the Soul®

I love your book. I put it to use immediately! (Even before I took it to work.) My next door neighbor called to talk because she had been worrying about her family financial situation for several months and it was affecting her health. I picked up my mail on the way to her house and started reading *Bounce Back!* while I waited for her to answer the door. Wow! The answer came in the mail. (Good things come in small packages.) We began our discussion using your definition of worrying. We laughed and it helped us both. By the way, "Dismantle The Box" is my favorite part of the book.

Jackie Johnson, Diversity Consultant
The Solutions Consulting Group

Bounce Back! is a wonderful book! I read it last night in the parking lot of the skating rink while I waited for my son and his friends. Your book inspired some real belly laughs and brightened my attitude immediately. I especially enjoyed "How to Worry — from an old family recipe." So funny, and so wise.

When I went into the skating rink to pick up my gang of skaters, I tried out the "Heart Step Two" technique and experienced the effects right away — I felt confident and happy and was greeted warmly by both kids and adults. (I'm sure the Honk techniques I'd been practicing in the car helped, too.)

Mary Griffith, Graphic Designer
Self-Employed

The *Bounce Back!* music CD is a gas! It made me want to dance (and I don't dance). Thanks for making me laugh.

Jerry Mullins, Landscape Contractor
J.M. Landscaping

*This book is dedicated
to all the children
who are my teachers
and my inspiration.*

Acknowledgments

Thank you to everyone who helped me with this book!

Everyone Who Read it and Gave Me Comments:
Matt Ahern, Susan Ahern, Fred Cook, Richard Deem, Melissa Demetrikopoulos, Jeffrey Ellis, Susana Escalante, Lee Glickstein, Annette Goodheart, Mary Grasberg, Dorit Har, Mark Hoge, Jackie Johnson, Laura Kristal, Karen Launier, Mary Leahy, Diana Luppi, Diana Lyon, Paula Marlatt, Stephanie Miyashiro, Mikel Newman, Emily Oldak, Julie Onstott, Glenda O'Rourke, Neshama Abraham Paiss, Zev Paiss, Pamela Rasmussen, Robyn, Dennis Shaver, Doug Shultz, Gloria Weissman, Debra Whitehead

My Teachers:
Robert Abramson, Bay Area Theatresports, Joe Bellan, Jeffrey Bihr, Adele Chu, Vickie Dodd, Steven Gunther, Melinda Harrison, Jan Henderson, Nancy Houfek, Marcia Kimmel, Seth Kimmelman, Joah Lowe, Joan Mankin, Randall McClellan, Melissa Michaels, Rhiannon, Bob Wells, Mr. Wooster

Improv Partners, Past and Present:
Wendy Davis, Doug Ettelson, Shelley Gefter, Lee Glickstein, Brett Isom, Laura Kristal, Ira Liss, Chrystos Minot, Steven Morris, Nick Peterson, Robert Power, Mark Pritchard, Saffire, the Singing Mimes

My Speaking Circle:
Jan Deville, Kate Fotopoulos, Ramone Yaciuk

The Production Team:
Char Campbell, George Foster, Mary Grasberg, Chrystos Minot, Jonathan and Maurissa Morningstar, Steven Morris, Tod Puck Wills

Special thanks to my publishers, Jonathan and Maurissa Morningstar, for believing in me and bouncing back over and over and over again.

The New Play Ethic at Work

Map of the Book

Welcome to **_Bounce Back!_**
Here's the secret key to what it's all about:

The Set-Up

Part 1 Defines terms like security and worrying as well as alternatives to worrying like — (Shhh! This is top secret, classified information for everybody except you and me) — HUMOR.

The Problem

Part 2 Reviews how we adults learned to worry so well and what some of the costs have been.

The Solution

Part 3 Explores the Play Ethic as a replacement for the Work and Worry Ethic.

The Personal Technology

Part 4 Provides practical humor activation techniques to help you stop worrying.

The Business Application

Part 5 Shows you how to create a productive, playful work environment where you can have FUN and get things done.

Lynn

Introduction

Healing Your *AMUSE* System

Bounce Back!

Just Add an F

During the earthquake of 1989, I was just finishing a 13-year sojourn in San Francisco. At that time, someone produced a bumper sticker stating, "SHIFT HAPPENS." They added one little "f" to an already popular slogan, and VOILA! It was a whole new way to look at things.

It's easy to get overwhelmed by change. Sometimes it's easier to think of it as excrement instead of opportunity. But just add that one little "f" (let's pretend it stands for FUN) and you're operating in a different world.

Pick Your Metaphor

A pile of poop or a pile of possibilities, you get to pick the way you view your life and act accordingly.

Healing Your *AMUSE* System

Most adults have suppressed Amuse systems. We don't really think anything is very funny. Certainly not when disaster strikes.

But, it is precisely at those times that we need to clear our minds and activate all of our inner resources. We need humor as an ally to connect to ourselves, the people around us and our world.

I first used "Healing Your Amuse System" as a workshop title during the rise of the AIDS epidemic in San Francisco when I was teaching and performing comedy with my friend, Lee Glickstein. Our response to AIDS in our community was to lead humor workshops for people living with AIDS, as well as their partners and their caregivers. We also led workshops called Laugh Tanks for people who were not necessarily dealing with life-threatening illnesses; people who just wanted to improve the quality of their lives and laugh more.

At the time, I also ran the San Francisco School of ReMirthing where I taught other classes about humor and healing.

Out of Commission

All this came to an abrupt halt when I hit a major depression. This is devastating for anyone. For a humorist, it's a major disability. I discontinued all my work while I went into an extended period of personal healing.

As I came through it, I learned to laugh from an even deeper place.

Back in the Game

I am grateful for this preparation and what I am able to share as we all face the task of **Bouncing Back** from recent traumatic events.

When the going gets tough, the tough start laughing. Change is a given. How we surf, fly or roll down the hill with it is a choice.

"Therefore, choose laugh."
I Say Uh, Chapter One, Verse One

Lynn Grasberg, Pagosa Springs, CO
September 2001

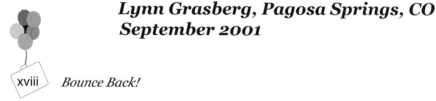

Bounce Back!

"For you shall go out with joy,
and be led forth with peace.
The mountains and hills shall break forth
before you into singing,
And all the trees of the field
shall clap their hands."
Isaiah, Chapter 55, Verse 12

Bounce Back!

Part 1

Confessions
of a
Corporate Clown

(and Recovering Worryholic)

Bounce Back!

Security
and
Other Modern Fairytales

𝕺nce upon a time,
not so long ago and not so far away,
people could count on jobs, families,
communities, even marriages
lasting their whole lives.

REALITY CHECK:

Maybe you've been down-sized, "right" sized, excised, out-sourced or undercut. You don't know if your job or even your company will still be there next year, let alone next Monday. Things we used to think were solid and eternal (like mutual funds, weather patterns, and our ability to remember things) shift and dissolve. You're probably worried about this.

This book is about how to STOP WORRYING and instead, develop the internal and interpersonal skills that provide our only real security as everything around us goes **cuckoo nuttiburgers** (to use the technical term).

Security:

a) The sense that all is well.
b) The illusion of permanence.
c) (Plural) Stocks and bonds.
   Financial instruments that people
   once pinned their hopes of (a) and
   delusions of (b) upon.

Security

is no longer something that can be supplied by external circumstances.*

*Perhaps it never could, except in our imaginations.

Our technology-accelerated
world is teaching us that
**we can only find security
within ourselves**
by learning to
shift with the winds,
roll with the tides,
surf the waves of change
and cultivate reliable
crewmates.*

* Are you getting seasick yet?
More ocean metaphors to follow.

Bounce Back!

Says Who?

Says me. I'm an expert at dealing with unpredictable events and circumstances.

I'll lay my credentials on the table: I'm a recovering worryholic. I'm also a professional clown, speaker/consultant and humorist. That means I take humor seriously.

April Fool!

I was partially prepared for this career path by my birthday — April Fool's Day. Fate dealt me a hand that required me to learn flexibility and non-abusive humor or be plagued by cruel jokes for the rest of my life. For example, someone gave me a big, beautifully wrapped box of gravel for my sixth birthday, hahaha. Ouch!

Parental Worrymeisters

I was also prepared for this career by my parents, both of whom were world-class worriers. I perfected the art of worrying, combining the "best" of my parents' styles (analytical, left-brained engineer and intuitive, right-brained nursery-school teacher).

I decided to unlearn this family trait when my parents died at the ages of 48 (father) and 53 (mother) due to several stress-related diseases.

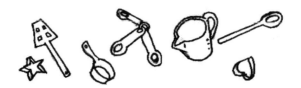

How to Worry

From an old family recipe

1. Pick a topic (any topic).

2. Imagine something bad happening in relation to that topic.

3. Replay this negative scenario over and over again in your mind.

4. As you replay this AWFUL THING (whatever it is), breathe very shallowly or, for maximum discomfort, stop breathing altogether.

5. Simultaneously, hold your body completely still while you:

6. Furrow your brow and clench some muscles.

7. Think, "It's hopeless. I'll never be able to handle this."

8. ***DO NOT, under any circumstances,***
   a. Breathe deeply.
   b. Move your body.
   c. Laugh.
   d. Ask for help.
   e. Problem-solve with one or more sympathetic human beings.
   f. Take concrete action.

Bounce Back!

Worrying:

The attempt to solve problems in the future by tormenting oneself *now* about possible bad results *then*.

Pseudo-Work

Worrying is pseudo-work. It allows you to feel like you are doing something useful while you're not actually getting anything done at all.

Worrying is more exhausting than real activity. It ties up your brain circuits which could be involved with more pleasurable and productive pursuits.

Bad Advice

People tell you not to worry because you'll make yourself sick. This is, of course, a useless piece of advice because if you worry about the fact that you worry, you'll make yourself *sicker*.

Ending the Worry Cycle

So stop worrying about worrying. My research shows that one way to break out of the cycle of anxiety and inaction is to CELEBRATE the very act of worrying. This gets you off the worry wheel, because it distracts you from future preoccupations and gets you actively doing something right now.

This, of course, is only one technique. But I'm giving it to you first because it WORKS — anything that might make you laugh and help you pay attention to something other than doom and gloom is worth a try. Right?

The following song is my tribute to worrying and a related condition — procrastination!

Putting Off the Rest*
(The Worry Song)
Song lyrics are on the next page.

Indication: Any or all of the following symptoms:
Clenched jaw, hands, shoulder
blades, buttocks, and/or brow;
face stuck in grimace;
fear stuck in pit of stomach;
free-floating feeling of doom
and/or gloom.

Application: 1. Hum along with the song
or
2. Sing the chorus mindlessly over
and over and over again
or
3. Sing the whole thing at the top of
your lungs.

* Each song in the book comes with a prescription including
indications (why you might need it) and applications (what
to do with it).

*The songs in this book are available on
the **Bounce Back!** music CD
if you would like to sing or hum along.*

*To order the **Bounce Back!** music CD and get a $5 discount
plus FREE shipping, go to www.bounceback.biz/CD.*

*You can also download free sheet music of
the songs from www.bounceback.biz.*

Putting Off the Rest
(The Worry Song)

Words and Music by Lynn Grasberg

1. I've got a list, a list of things,
   A list of things to do,
   Tasks and projects, big ideas,
   A very ambitious brew.
   Well, the list keeps getting longer
   While my attention is so short,
   Except, of course, for worrying
   'Cuz that's my favorite sport.

Chorus: Worrying's not on the list
         But it's the thing that I do best.
         It's the job that I'm perfecting
         While I'm putting off the rest.

2. I've been told I could be happy
   If I'd just apply myself,
   But I spend all my energy
   Just sitting on the shelf,
   Caught between the voice that says,
   "You must!" and
   "You better watch out or you'll be a bust!"
   So I never take that fateful leap
   Even though I'm losing so much sleep.
   I've a midnight worry date to keep . . .
   It's an appointment I can trust.
                                    Chorus

3. Someday I'll leave behind my angst
   And join the more successful ranks
   Of people who check off all their lists,
   Whose deadlines are never ever missed.
   Who, when asked for their philosophy,
   Will insist,
   "Just don't THINK and you won't resist."
                                    Chorus

Bounce Back!

4. Oh, resistance is my business,
   "I don't wanna!" is my creed.
   It's an affirmation that's stuck by me
   Through my every hour of need.
   Some people say it's too negative
   But I know it's the best
   'Cuz it really keeps me going
   While I'm putting off the rest.
                          Chorus

© Lynn Grasberg 1987

Corporate Clown

I sang that song for a long time and eventually, I embraced my destiny. I became a clown, Penelope the Clown, to be specific.

I have been known to show up for business meetings, conferences and even keynote speeches in less than formal attire. (Big red nose, turquoise high top sneakers and rainbow eyelashes do not meet the dress code of most business organizations.)

I have also been known to pass as a serious adult by toning down my look but I'm really just working undercover at those times as a ***Plain Nose Clown.***

Plain Nose Clown:

Undercover humor activator.

Someone who is empowered to raise the humor level, and therefore, the level of functionality and intelligence, wherever they go.

[See Official Clown Permit, p. 61.]

My Mission

I wear whatever it takes to get my foot in the door because I'm on a serious mission —

To help adults recover their ability to laugh and play together in order to:

- Stop worrying.
- Honor and cherish all children *including the child that lives inside each grown-up.*
- Make better decisions and policies under rapidly changing conditions.
- Work together more harmoniously.
- Have FUN while getting things done.

> # Fun is not frivolous.
> ## The human animal is most intelligent when playing.

"So, What Exactly Do You Do?"

People are always asking me what I do for a living. Since what I do doesn't fit into traditional job descriptions, I've come up with my own. Here are my top four. Take your pick:

1. **ReMirther:** One who restores humor if it's been lost or misplaced.

2. **Corporate Clown:** One who is willing to sacrifice dignity, propriety and "appropriate" behaviors in order to bring out the intelligence and compassion of an organization and its members.

3. **Non-Toxic Comic:** One who invokes laughter without toxic by-products (cruelty, humiliation, alienation, etc.)

4. **Humor Relations Consultant:** One who coaches individuals, teams and organizations to become more effective and resilient by developing interactive humor skills and an attitude of productive playfulness.

Bounce Back!

Inclusive Humor

I specialize in inclusive humor — the kind that means everybody "gets the joke" and no one is the butt of it. *Inclusive* humor connects people and promotes collaboration.

In contrast, *abusive* ("put-down") humor evokes laughter at someone else's expense and contributes to an atmosphere of veiled criticism, fear and isolation.

Make Up Your Own

In these times of change (i.e., the rest of our lives), more and more of us will be creating our own jobs instead of "looking" for them.

You need to have something to put on your business cards. So, why not make up your own job title like I did? Since you define it yourself, no one can fire you and you get to change the job description as needed!

Why Did the Humorist Cross the Road?

Q: Why did the humorist cross the road?

A: Wasn't it a chicken?

Q: It doesn't really matter.

A: It doesn't?

Q: No.

A: What was the question?

Q: Why did the CHICKEN cross the road?

A: Didn't you say humorist?

Q: It doesn't matter! Why did the chicken cross the road?

A: I might be able to answer that if you could tell me what was on the other side.

Q: I don't know. Nothing.

A: The chicken crossed the road for nothing?

Q: No — to get to the other side! That's the way the joke goes.

A: But why would the chicken cross the road to get to nothing?

Q: You're missing the point.

A: I am?

Q: Yeah. And you keep answering questions with questions instead of answers.

A: I do?

Q: You just did it again!

A: So?

Q;   So — I'm Q. I'm supposed to ask the questions. You're A. You're supposed to answer them.

A: Where did all these rules come from?

Q: Stop it with the questions. Where did YOU come from?

A: Brawk!

Navigating with Humor
(I told you we'd get back to the ocean.)

A healthy sense of humor is essential for navigating the ocean of life, death and bad metaphors. Humor helps us have **perspective** on our tragi-comic dramas. Not to mention, boring meetings.

Ah, perspective. So easy to lose while multi-tasking in the muck.

We all have the ability to shift our perspective, although sometimes it feels like we need a two-ton truck to help move us when we get stuck. Humans are amazing though. We can do it, especially with practice. Humor helps.

Nobody is required to
be a victim to his or
her own bad attitude.

Flexibility

Our ability to flexibly shift our viewpoints is a learnable skill that has positive repercussions on our health, our ability to communicate with difficult people (especially ourselves) and our capacity to solve "impossible problems."

Seasickness
and
Other Occupational Hazards

This book is the result of my journey as a recovering worryholic. "Seasick" is too mild a term for how it's felt during major parts of this ongoing voyage. However, I've learned to trust my own judgment, laugh at my own jokes and shift my perspective even while things are falling apart around me.

As a recovering worryholic, I've learned to enjoy my own pratfalls as *comic* moments instead of big tragedies. At least, most of the time.

News Flash!

Things will continue to fall apart
during our lifetimes.
We don't have to fall apart ourselves,
at least not all the time.

Bounce Back!
Humor and Resilience

What follows are ideas and practices to restore perspective, maintain health and develop robust individuals and organizations that thrive on change. Here we go! Wheeeeeee . . .!

Bounce Back:

The ability to quickly recover from (and even enjoy) challenges that previously knocked you for a loop.

You are cordially invited to
STOP WORRYING
and reclaim your ability to
BOUNCE BACK
and enjoy your life.

Bounce Back!

Part 2

But Seriously, Folks
How We Learn to Worry
All the Time

Bounce Back!

Don't Look at Your Friend!

Think back to third grade. You and your classmates are sitting in hard little seats in orderly rows listening to your teacher follow an orderly lesson plan. Don't look at your friend! If you do, both of you will burst out laughing and the teacher will get mad and everybody will stare at you. You are a good kid, but . . . you can't help it and you are laughing hysterically.

What's So Funny?

"Would you like to share what's so funny with the whole class?" Nope. You can't because you'll get in even more trouble. Or maybe you don't even have words to say what made you laugh. It's just your natural silliness and energy bursting out. Something the teacher said struck you as funny, or maybe it's the way your friend crossed her eyes, or . . . it doesn't really matter. You're in trouble.

Witnesses in Hell

Maybe you're not even the one laughing. Maybe you're one of the other young people quietly sitting at your desk watching this happen to someone else. But you're in trouble too. Everything stops for the public humiliation of those who DARE to break up their boredom with laughter. You decide this will never happen to you.

You will learn to "control yourself."

Act Your Age!

Before this momentous (and I would say, traumatic) decision, you were a free-wheeling, playful person. I'm sure you held out as long as you possibly could, but eventually you gave in to pressures to "act your age."

Some of us were "precocious" and even became quiet and serious— so mature! — as BABIES.

Do the Math

A typical four year old laughs FOUR HUNDRED times a day. A typical "grown-up" laughs MAYBE 15 times a day. And those aren't all big belly laughs. A lot of those are nervous little laughs of suppressed embarrassment.

Do the math. 400 minus 15 equals why you are such a bundle of nerves and gas. Luckily, lost laughs are retrievable.

Revision

Phooey! I should have called the preceding page "Do the Research." I've been quoting these numbers for YEARS and they're *so catchy*. I wanted to give credit where credit is due (exactly who went around counting all those laughs?) so I looked it up on the Internet.

I found HUNDREDS of articles that quoted these numbers but guess what! Lots and lots of people say, "Studies show that . . ." or "Research shows . . ." but NOBODY cited an actual study. So, due to lack of documentation, at least at this time, the closest I can get to a "fact" about this is:

"A typical four year old laughs a whole lot. A typical 'grown-up' laughs a whole lot less."

Not as punchy. But hard to argue with.

Bounce Back!

Warning:

The next two pages are NOT FUNNY. They are about how many of us got hurt when we were very young. Feel free to skip them if you are sensitive to violence and tune back in on page 46.

Cuz I Said So, That's Why

Q: Hey you! What's so funny?

A: Nothing.

Q: Then wipe that silly grin off your face.

A: Why?

Q: There you go with the questions again.

A: But why shouldn't I smile?

Q: Because no one will take you seriously if you look like that.

A: Who says?

Q: Me. I'm bigger, older and more experienced than you.

A: So?

Q: So I said wipe that smile off your face.

A: Why?

Q: Cuz I said so, that's why.

A: Why?

Q: Cuz I said so! (Smack!)

Bounce Back!

A: (Rubbing sore spot on head)
Oh, I get it.

Q: I knew you would.

A: Yeah, being serious all the time is REALLY stupid.

Q: That's not what I meant.

A: That's cuz you're stupid.

Q: Watch it!

A: (Dodging a blow)
Yup! You think you're smarter cuz you're serious and mean.

Q: I'll show you mean! (Smack!)

A: (Crying) Stupid!

Q: (Smack!) Who's stupid now?

A: Nobody.

Q: (Smack!) Who?

A: Me.

Q: Now we're getting somewhere.

A: (Whispered) Stupid.

Stupid:

Not able to access one's full intelligence due to insult and injury one has not recovered from yet. In this sense, worrying is a "stupid" activity.

Sources of
Humor Impairment

Fear of
   Embarrassment
   Humiliation
   Disapproval
   Punishment/Physical Pain
   Looking
      stupid
      foolish
      dumb
      dopey
      weird . . .
   Being judged as
      bad
      wrong
      sinful
      immature
      irresponsible . . .

Energy Drain

No wonder grown-ups drag around so much! It takes a lot of energy to try to avoid all the stuff listed on the preceding page.

Laugh Depletion

Not only are we tired. We suffer from a serious depletion of laughter and joy.

How did we go from several barrels of laughs a day to a feeble handful? We were subjected to lots of "Shut up and sit down!" and "Wipe that stupid smile off your face!" and "Big boys don't cry," and "Nice girls don't get angry."

Laughing, crying, yelling and fabulous exuberance are not just for the very young. But most of us learned our lessons too well.

Serious Adult Syndrome

Once you learn to suppress yourself, you are well on your way to being considered an adult in our culture. In fact, a key proof that you are "mature" is how well you worry. It increases your credibility and stature in the community of serious-minded folk.

However, habitual worrying has a downside. It leads to SAS or Serious Adult Syndrome.

SAS is actually a life-threatening condition! It contributes to heart disease, cancer, immune system suppression and every other stress-related malady you can think of. It also makes us stupid.

Woe Is We: Some Serious Statistics

You KNOW worrying is bad for you. Do you need some statistics? Okay, take your pick. One out of every ten, 47%, and 751/800ths. There! Do you feel better? I didn't think so.

Some Serious Facts

Worrying is about holding still and feeling bad. Stuck. Paralyzed. Unable to act and unable to stop thinking about your problems. And thinking and thinking and . . .

A Glimmer of Hope

What can be done to reverse the debilitating effects of worrying and SAS? To quote Uncle Albert from *Mary Poppins*, laugh "long and loud and clear."

Parts 3 and 4 cover humor principles and techniques to help you undo the deadly effects of SAS, reclaim your birthright as a brilliant, playful person and become a master at handling change.

Humor:

A healthy perspective. The ability to notice the difference between what IS and "what's sposed to be" . . . and find it amusing.

Life is Life

Song lyrics are on the next page.

Indication: When your mind is stuck on "tragic" thoughts, i.e., "I'm gonna lose, no matter what, so why bother?"

Application: 1. Sing the first verse mindlessly over and over and over and over and over and over again.
2. When you're feeling better, dance around and belt out the whole thing.

Life is Life

Words and Music by Lynn Grasberg

1. Life is life.
   Why is why.
   Cuz is cuz,
   And it's all is.

2. Life is huh?
   Why is I dunno.
   Cuz is cuz,
   And it's all so.

3. Life is life.
   Why is la-la-la.
   Cuz is oh!
   And it's all Ahhhh.

4. Life is oops!
   Why is hee h' hee.
   Cuz is ha!
   And it's all Wheeee!

© Lynn Grasberg 2001
(Revised version)

Part 3

Play as You Go

The Antidote to Worry

Bounce Back!

Good Job!

You did a good job of learning the complex task of worrying. Feel free to pat yourself on the back.

JUST BECAUSE YOU'RE GOOD AT IT DOESN'T MEAN YOU HAVE TO KEEP DOING IT!

There is an alternative. The antidote to worrying is (Ta-DAH!) to be playful.

Playful:

Flexible and intelligent. Available to engage with whatever is going on in the moment; poised for fun.

The Work Ethic (Review)

For those of you who just dropped in from another planet, I'll review the Work Ethic that runs — and ruins — many lives.

1. Work hard now
   so you can
2. Save money now
   so you can
3. Stop working later
   so you can
4. Rest and have some fun later,
   and/or
5. Die.

The Play Ethic
(Don't Wait to Retire)

There's another way to live and work. As the Work Ethic gives way to the Play Ethic, here are the new rules:

Play as you go.
1. Take time for rest and fun now
      so you can
2. Enjoy your work now
      so you can
3. Have more energy now
      so you can
4. Enjoy your life now
      AND
5. Still enjoy it when you're older.

Permission

In case you encounter difficulties with people who have not yet switched over to the Play Ethic, I have included a Practice Permit. Feel free to copy it and carry it with you at all times. If you act on it, you have deputized yourself as a Plain Nose Clown.

Official Clown Permit
(Permanent Permission Slip)

This permit permits the permit bearer to:
• Play with anyone in the whole world,
• Commit bold acts of silliness and surprise,
• Care about others with shameless exuberance and
• Laugh out loud. HA!

No expiration date.
Automatically applies to anyone who sees, touches, hears about or spontaneously imagines this card.

Life and Laughter:
Seven Assumptions

1. **Human beings are naturally playful and glad to be alive.**
   Need proof? Observe a baby who has his or her basic needs met — food, shelter, rest, physical safety, clean diaper, being held and talked to with awareness and affection. (Our needs don't really change that much as we get older, do they?)

2. **Most adults are humor-impaired to some degree.**
   Mostly due to fear of embarrassment. See Part 2.

3. **We didn't start out that way.**
   See #1 above.

4. **We can all reclaim our playfulness, humor and delight.**
   With a little encouragement.

5. **We handle change much more easily when we are playful.**
   Playing with more possibilities leads to better solutions and a repertoire of ways to handle all kinds of situations that we would never come up with if we were trying to follow a narrow, rigid code of thinking and behaving.

6. **We don't really know anything for sure.**
   We make ourselves miserable when we feel we have to.

7. **That's okay.**
   After all, life is a mystery and a miracle. How can you understand all that? Might as well start laughing now!

The Peekaboo Path:
Learning from the Masters

Babies are masters of humor. And they don't know any jokes yet. But they are hard-wired for the most basic human game: peekaboo.

Who says babies have short attention spans? If you've played peekaboo with one recently, you know that the baby will wear YOU out before he or she gets tired of the game.

The truth is, babies have short attention spans for activities that are not intrinsically interesting. But peekaboo is fascinating.

Peekaboo: A Refresher Course

Peekaboo basics:

Connection, separation, reconnection.

Peekaboo is the basis of all of our great literature and spiritual traditions. Peekaboo is IT! in the world of entertainment and enlightenment.

How to play:

First, one of us covers our eyes and PRETENDS the other person (and maybe even the whole world) has gone away. Then, with just the right comic timing, we move our hands or heads, and . . . we're both still here! And we laugh and laugh with relief and delight because we haven't really lost each other.

Beyond Isolation

When we play peekaboo, we get to laugh about our fear of being abandoned and the illusion that we're all alone.

Even though we're no longer babies (at least on the outside), we still need reassurance that we're really here, that we're connected to other people, and that we matter.

That's why I'm a fan of inclusive humor — the practice of sharing humor through connection and the shock of mutual recognition.

Inclusive Humor:

Humor that connects from the heart; the shared appreciation of the absurdities of life.

Recovering Connection

Sometimes, in our adult interactions, we "can't see" each other. We lose connection and react to our anger or fear instead of the other person who is actually with us.

To reconnect, use the wisdom of Peekaboo: Open your eyes! Move your hands! Peek around the other person's hands! Reach out.

Peekaboo Strategies for Reconnecting:

Open your eyes.
Notice the other person — their eyes, their nose, the color of their shirt — anything about them that will remind you there's a real person there.

Move your hands.
Make a distinction between the "problem" (the hands covering one or both of your eyes) and the participants. Either or both of you can move your own hands to see things from a different perspective.

Peek around the other person's hands.
If the other person is upset, peek around their agitation to find the human.

It's all about reaching out and including each other. To help in this process, here are 10 principles of Inclusive Humor (Advanced Peekaboo).

🎯 Principles of Inclusive Humor

1. Include yourself.

2. Include everyone else.

3. Include the given circumstances.

4. Practice *Yes-and.*

5. Choose your perspective: comedy or tragedy.

6. See the world through innocent eyes.

7. Observe humor at all energy levels.

8. Look for humor so it can find you.

9. Amplify humor with your awareness.

10. Recognize jokes as accessories, not necessities.

Include Yourself

This is the most important principle.

The FIRST person you need to connect with is yourself. (See Part 4, *Raise Your HQ*, for specific suggestions.)

In stressful situations, it's common to abandon yourself. Then it seems as if you are living in a tragic universe where nobody is there for you. And when that nobody is YOU, it feels really dismal.

Compassion starts at home. Including yourself means deciding that you, like everyone else, deserve kindness, practical assistance and moral support. Including yourself means that you organize your circumstances to make sure you get these things.

When you include yourself, you have access to a lot more possibilities for action and connection to other people.

Include Everyone Else

In other words, notice that you're not the only one here. There are all kinds of people in the world and life gets richer when you notice the humanity reflected in everyone, even the ones you consider "different" from yourself.

When you expand your perspective to include others, things get funnier and everything lightens up around you. Peekaboo!

"It's all done with people."

Have you ever been in a Fun House at a carnival? It's filled with distorting mirrors. You can look in one and see a version of yourself that's extremely short and fat. Another mirror makes you look tall and skinny. As they say in the carnival world, "It's all done with mirrors."

Now flip the looking glass. See that your reflection in this Fun House world we live in is "all done with people." Mirrors need people or there'd be no reflections. And we're all mirrors for each other.

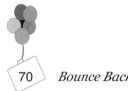

Include the Given Circumstances
Welcome the unknown.

We really don't know what's going to happen next even though we'd really like to, and we'd like to know it's something we want, and we'd love to be able to control it, whatever it is.

HOWEVER . . .
We can't.

THEREFORE, we have more power in each moment when we welcome it and see what it holds for us. This goes against lots of training to try and control things.

At first, when you welcome the unknown, you may experience a little fear. (How's that for an understatement!) Just breathe through it and keep your eyes open.

You never know what might show up!

Practice *Yes-and*
Accept gifts and make offers.

This is an expansion of Principle #3.

Accept the gifts of the moment (the given circumstances) by saying **Yes!**
Then, build on them with **and . . .**

For example, if someone says, "Wanna hear the idea I had for improving our micro-widget?" you can kill the conversation with "Not really," or "Yes, but nobody's interested in any new ideas around here." In both cases, you are *blocking* the flow of possibility and creativity.

Let's take that over again with a *Yes-and* approach.

"Wanna hear the idea I had for improving our micro-widget?"

"Yes, and I'd like to see how it works with the mini-gizmo that I put together with Mary."

"Great idea! Maybe we can combine them into a super-mini-widget gizmo."

The *Yes-and* Advantage

Yes-and is a mind-opening attitude (as compared to "Yes, but..." or "No, because..."). It's the basis of high-level collaboration and is the primary principle of ***Improvisation*** — the art and science of spontaneous problem-solving.

I could write a whole book on THIS one . . . and I will! In the meantime, I highly recommend *IMPRO*, the classic book on improvisation by Keith Johnstone.

Choose Your Perspective
Comedy or Tragedy?

> "Just because you're miserable doesn't mean
> you can't enjoy your life."
> — Annette Goodheart, author of *Laughter Therapy*

In classical literature, tragedy is when the hero or she-ro (that's the female protagonist) loses (usually dies) because of a "fatal flaw." In comedy, the s/hero has just as many flaws as in a tragedy, but gets to win in the end anyway.

In your own life, you get to choose your attitude: are you winning or losing? Do you treat moments of adversity as opportunities to reach out to other people and resources, or as occasions to retreat and moan, "Why me?"

Actually, if you can ask "Why me?" and answer, "Because I'm the one who can handle it!" you're on your way to being a comic s/hero.*

*Of course, this does not mean you have to squish any feelings that come up that are less than heroic. It's fine to feel sad, angry, scared or _____. (Fill in the blank.) Just remember principle #1 (**Include Yourself**) and don't abandon yourself while you're feeling any of your emotions.

See the World
Through Innocent Eyes

The world is full of surprises, information and unexpected gifts when you look at it with innocent eyes.

Welcome to the realm of clowns and babies. They observe the world with innocent eyes, without immediately categorizing everything as good or bad, or by its usual function.

Decide to be a scientist of the heart — one who sees everything as something to explore, to examine without judging it, and, in the case of a real baby, to put in the mouth.

Of course, some of the stuff "out there" is painful or unpleasant. That's why it's important to also have your adult self on duty, the one that witnesses and remembers that fire burns and sharp things hurt. Make sure the innocent-eyed one is accompanied by your inner adult guardian so you can enjoy the world as surprising and entertaining as it really is.

Enjoy Humor at all Energy Levels

Some people think that humor is only worth noting when it's a big belly laugh or you laugh so hard you almost pee in your pants.

But humor exists in very quiet and subtle ways too. They all count:

- Something that makes you smile, like the sparkle of a rainbow in a drop of dew in the grass. That counts.

- Your delight in finding one more french fry hiding under a piece of lettuce when you thought they were all gone. That counts.

- The silliness when your 3-year old notices you put your shirt on backwards and you both giggle. That counts.

From mildest Mona Lisa smile to biggest guffaw, it all counts.

Look for Humor So It Can Find You

Isn't it amazing how different the world looks, depending on what you are paying attention to? There's funny stuff happening all around you all the time, but you can miss it completely if you're not paying attention. Then it's like that tree falling in the forest with no one to hear it. It doesn't really exist for you unless you notice it. Once you decide to, be prepared to walk around in a state of incipient delight.

This is what I call having a well-functioning *AMUSE* System.

Amplify Humor with Your Attention

There's an old adage that says, "Whatever you give energy to, increases." Your readiness to notice and appreciate humor multiplies the effect of what's already there and attracts more.

The twinkle in your eye and your willingness to laugh literally INCREASES the humor in your environment.

Recognize Jokes as Accessories, not Necessities

"Jokes are just by-products of the humor process."
— Lee Glickstein, author of *Be Heard Now!*

Can't remember jokes? Don't worry about it. Your sense of humor is not dependent on your memory. (Isn't that a relief?) The funniest stuff is what comes up in the moment.

Jokes are a tiny subset of humor. If you enjoy them, great. If you don't, just tune into the cosmic giggle and join in.

Perks of the Playful Path

Practicing the Play Ethic is SERIOUSLY better for your health, productivity and general well-being. Play as you go and you don't have to burn out!

A Few Health Benefits

Medical studies show that laughing and maintaining a generally playful attitude can:

- Lower blood pressure.
- Decrease pain.
- Increase immune function.
- Decrease allergic reactions.

You can find an excellent bibliography on the health effects of humor and laughter in Patch Adams' book, *Gesundheit!*

I also highly recommend, *Laughter Therapy* by Annette Goodheart, and the granddaddy of all books on the subject, *Anatomy of an Illness* by Norman Cousins.

Humor Yourself

"We don't laugh because we are happy.
We are happy because we laugh."

— William James

When you laugh, amazing things happen in your body. For one thing, your pituitary gland sends endorphins into your bloodstream. Endorphins are the body's built-in pleasure chemicals and pain relievers. Your body naturally regulates them so, unlike drugs or alcohol, there are no side effects or withdrawal symptoms to suffer through later.

Natural Detox

You get a lot of the same health benefits from crying as you do from laughing. (Ever notice how you feel more balanced and peaceful after a good cry — the kind where you really "let it out?")

Laughter is one of many forms of release (including crying, shaking, sweating and yawning) that help you eliminate toxins, heal emotional injuries, recharge your batteries and think more clearly. Laughing just happens to be the most accessible one for many of us and the one we associate most with FUN.

How Can I Get More of These Endorphins?

Turn to Part 4 to jumpstart more laughter and creativity in your life.

Meanwhile, would you care to dance?

Samba on the Ceiling

Song lyrics are on the next page.

Indication: When you need to maintain humor under circumstances that might otherwise suppress, repress, oppress or depress you.

Application: (Harsh circumstances)
        Think it and grin inside.
  (Moderate)
        Hum it and snicker.
  (Relaxed)
        Kick off your shoes and dance.

P.S. I apologize for the gender-specific clothing mentioned in the song. Feel free to modify it to suit your own wardrobe.

♪ Samba on the Ceiling

Words and Music by Lynn Grasberg

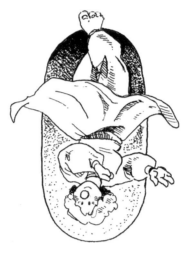

I'm willing to wear this makeup
And even these stupid high heels,
And for awhile I'll go out and smile
And make some business deals.

But even as I'm playing this role,
It's not really of my whole soul
Which is busy dancing
On the ceiling,
Doing the samba in bare feet,
Being so discreet
That no one else can see
And I can still be me.

©Lynn Grasberg 1990

*To order the **Bounce Back!** music CD and
get a $5 discount plus FREE shipping,
go to www.bounceback.biz/CD.*

Bounce Back!^{SM}

Part 4

Raise Your HQ*
Hands-on Techniques to Lift Your Spirits

*Humor Quotient

Bounce Back!

Roll Up Your Sleeves

Okay. This is the nuts and bolts, hands-on, how-to part. Specific techniques to activate your sense of play, humor and creativity.

Dismantle the Box

It's trendy to talk about thinking "outside the box." The implication is that as soon as one is done with that little session, one promptly crawls back INTO the box.

Fuhgeddaboudit! We can do better than that. MAYBE we'll be ready to spend time in boxes when we're dead. Until then, here are some techniques to bust down the walls and expand the playroom to include the whole world.

Warm UP!
A Toes to Nose Procedure

One reason that children laugh so much is that they have a lot of physical ENERGY. (Revelation: so do grown-ups; it's just hidden behind the fatigue.)

So, you gotta use your body (not just your mind, although it's good to bring that along too) to activate your humor. When your blood is moving and your breathing is freed up, it's much easier to laugh and have fun. Here's a toes to nose procedure to get you started.

Bounce Back!

Humor Activation Points

Nose

Heart

Belly button

Knees

start here>>   Toes

(Please stand up for the full effect of this warm-up.)

Toes

Wiggle your toes!

It's a tiny movement that affects your whole body and improves your mood.

It helps you feel your connection to the ground. Because you're moving SOMETHING, it breaks up the paralysis of fear or jitters of nervousness (especially if you're getting up to speak in front of other people or some other brave act like that). And, if you're wearing shoes, nobody else has to know what you're up to.

I was taught this technique by my clown friend, Aha Yahoo, the grand teacher of **Haha Yoga.**

Wiggle your toes.

It's simple. It's silly. It works.

Knees

Now, check your knees. Make sure they have a little bend, a little bounce.

Why? You'll find out if you do the opposite. Straighten your knees and hold them tight. Notice how your lower back tightens at the same time. This constricts your breathing and contributes to lower back pain, both major humor dampeners.

So put some spring in your knees. You have now completed step #2 of the warm-up process.

Belly Button

No, this is not about contemplating your navel (although, feel free to do that too). This is really about BREATHING, a prerequisite for having a good time.

What's your belly button got to do with it? If you're breathing fully and deeply (something we rarely do when we feel worried or tense), your belly button will be MOVING with each breath.

Pretend your belly is a big balloon that expands as it fills with air and shrinks as you let out that air. As you inhale, your belly button moves OUT and as you exhale, your belly button moves back IN.

If you really want to enjoy yourself, *sigh* on the outbreath. Ahhhhhhh . . .

Heart
Step One

Place your hands, one over the other, over the center of your chest. This is a universal gesture of comfort and you may feel soothed immediately. Now, hum into your hands (hmmmm). Amazing! Notice that your own voice is uniquely designed to calm you when you hum through your chest.

Heart
Step Two

Now, pretend you have a sun in the middle of your chest that radiates light. If you want to close it down, collapse your chest and hunch your shoulders. This is the "poor me" position. It's easy to feel bad when your body is scrunched like this.

If you want to open up and shine, stand tall, with your shoulders relaxed and back. This will automatically open your chest. If you walk about in this position and imagine sending out light from your heart, you'll notice it's easier to connect with and enjoy everyone and everything in your environment.

Bounce Back!

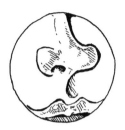

Nose

You're ready to activate the ultimate humor point: the shnoz, the nasal aperture, the place of smellification, the most exuberant part of clowns and dogs — THE NOSE!

The nose is inherently funny. In Chinese medicine, it's connected directly to the heart. So give it some attention: wiggle it, give it a hug* and notice that anything you point it at gets funnier. At least, it will soon.

* Nasal hug instructions on page 101.

Review

Okay. Let's go through that warm-up one more time:

Wiggle your toes.
Bounce your knees.
Breathe through your belly button.
Hum into your heart.
Shine light from the center of your chest.
Hug your nose.

Bounce Back!

From the Nose

Now you're ready for SERIOUS humor activation. For this, we must delve deeper into the nose (figuratively speaking, of course).

We'll be doing that digging in a moment in **Honk!** — the first of five humor techniques in the BounceBACK Office suite.

BounceBACK Office:

Five Humor Techniques

These techniques are designed to help you get out of an isolated funk and into humorous connection with yourself, other people and/or the universe (for those who are cosmically inclined).

The five techniques are:

Honk!
Develop a nose for humor.

This is a heavy-duty technique for those days when you wake up feeling lousy, worried or generally disinclined to get up and do anything. In other words, days when NOTHING IS FUNNY.

(Sometimes, of course, you might need to elevate your mood after you've been up and about for a while. In that case, you can initiate the HONK! later in the day at your discretion.)

There are five steps to mastering nasal humor: the Gaze, the Hug, Laffirmation, Nasal Massage, and the Feather.

1. THE GAZE
   Look in the mirror. (You're probably thinking,
   "This is supposed to cheer me up?" Please bear
   with me. Things will improve.)

   Look at your NOSE in the mirror. (This is
   generally more fun than scrutinizing yourself for
   pimples or wrinkles.) If you feel an incipient
   sneeze or giggle, let it out!

2. THE HUG (Moral Support)
   Appreciate your nose for leading the way all day
   and give it a little reassurance.

   How? Wrap your fingers around it and give it a
   hug. Like this:

Notice that it's hard to stay depressed while
looking at yourself hugging your nose.

3. LAFFIRMATION
   To further counteract the tendency to be mean
   and cranky when you feel bad, say nice things to
   yourself (affirmations) while you hug your nose.
   This turns them into *laffirmations.*

   For example, say, "You're looking very attractive
   today," and "What an intelligent person you are."
   You get the idea.

4. NASAL MASSAGE (external!)
   Now that you've reassured and grounded your nose, it's time to stimulate its ability to receive and amplify humor.

   With an index finger, massage the tip of your nose with a circular motion. Like this:

To balance the energy, reverse the direction:

When you take your finger away, notice a tingling or buzzing sensation in the tip of your nose. Your humor receptor/amplifier is activated! Anything or anyone you point it at will get funnier.

Try it first on your image in the mirror, then on other humans as well as miscellaneous objects as you go through your day.

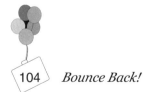

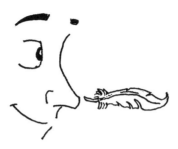

5. THE FEATHER (advanced technique)
   Imagine there is a feather at the end of your nose. It is infinitely extendable and instantly retractable.

   You can use it to deliver a gentle tickle and raise the humor level of people at great distances from yourself (for example, several cars over in a traffic jam or on the other side of a room during a meeting that is going on too long).

   Since your feather is invisible, you are now equipped to be a secret humor activator everywhere you go.

Variation

For maximum effect, try the Honk! technique with another person. I suggest you each treat the other person's FACE as your mirror. Be sure to look each other in the eyes. The Giggle Factor goes WAY up when you're looking at someone else hugging their nose, etc.

Warning!

Honk! (otherwise known as Nasal Humor Activation) is a very powerful technique. I trust you will use it with sensitivity and integrity. Because, as you know, with increased power goes increased responsibility:

Only YOU can decide where (and when) to point your *humor activated* nose.

Yoo-Hoo!
Connect with unlikely colleagues.

Reach up your hand, wiggle your fingers and say, "Yoo-Hoo!"

If you wave at someone as if you know them (even if you've never spoken before), it's uncanny how many will wave back at you (sometimes a bit confused).

"Have we met before?" they may ask.
"No, but I'm glad we have now."

As an experienced clown, I can tell you, that almost every young child will giggle and probably wave back at you. (They know this is just a variation of Peekaboo.)

Sometimes grown-ups are a tougher case. Luckily, behind that stern facade is a delightful person with a sense of humor (even if it's buried).

Yoo-Hoo Enhancement

Yoo-Hoo! combines well with Honk!, especially employing the feather technique to tickle people at a distance.

The Think Method

Yoo-Hoo is more of an attitude than a protocol. You don't always have to wave and say Yoo-Hoo. But if you THINK it as you approach people, you may be surprised at how many of them respond favorably.

What to Do with "Tough" Cases

Be persistent. Some people take a while to warm up.

There are many ways to invite another person to play. Although they may not look like it, even super-grumpy, ultra-serious people would like to join you. If you can hold an attitude of relaxed friendliness, despite the fact that someone is barking at you (I didn't say this was always easy), and if you don't give up, eventually you will find that person's sense of humor.

Consider yourself a permanent member of the welcoming committee.

Permanent Member
of the Welcoming Committee

Grumpy people usually are feeling isolated and unhappy. If you happen to fall into this category occasionally yourself, there's something YOU can do.

Don't be miserable, waiting for some kind of fairy godmother person to show up and invite you into the group. BE that person. Greet other people and create a warm environment for everybody. Then, guess what? You will have created an atmosphere that welcomes you too. Kindness and friendliness are actually contagious.

Be the one who welcomes and you will feel at home.

The Best

The following two techniques are the best things I learned when I went to clown school. Since most of you probably didn't go to clown school, I'm happy to share these remedial techniques with you. Once you start applying them, you may wish you learned them in kindergarten.

Oops!

Enjoy (and broadcast) your mistakes.

Most of us were taught that it's bad to make mistakes so we cover them up. Of course, this is VERY STRESSFUL and usually makes things worse.

Instead of minimizing your mistake, make a BIG deal out of it. Point it out with an enthusiastic "OOPS!" and enjoy the event with others rather than feel mortified by yourself.

The Oops Advantage

When you let other people know about your mistakes, you are more likely to get help. (You'll never get any help if it's a big secret. Besides, your willingness to show what's going on with you might open the door for other people to do the same.)

If you practice saying OOPS! when you don't need it, it's easier to remember when you do.

All together now:

OOPS!

Oops! Success Story

One of my biggest accomplishments in the Oops! arena was the time I fell down on a sidewalk and managed to hit the ground laughing. "Oops!" I bellowed through my own uproarious laughter. I laughed and laughed the way I used to when I was a baby learning to walk (falling down and getting up and falling down and getting up . . .).

I felt much better when I got up. And so did the kind stranger who gave me a hand. We both walked away laughing. It was much more satisfying than if I tried to act like "nothing happened."

Ta-DAH!
Celebrate EVERYTHING
(starting with yourself).

When you go to the circus (and admit it, doesn't your office sometimes seem like a circus?), there is a fine old tradition that we expect as audiences and that we NEED in order to feel that the show is complete. It's the applause part.

After someone does a death-defying feat or a ridiculous trick, they raise their arms, the music declares "Ta-DAH!" and everybody claps, sometimes even standing to do so.

Who Needs It?

(Applause, that is)

Everybody. We all need to be celebrated and appreciated.

There are times when each of us has done something great (like completing a report and delivering it ON TIME despite all kinds of obstacles). But no one knows because there was no Ta-DAH! — no signal for applause. We feel unappreciated and can't understand why we feel so tired.

There is nothing more energizing than appreciation so use Ta-DAH! to get the applause you deserve.

Asking for It

Here's how they do it in the circus.

1. Raise your arms wide and sing out
    "Ta-DAH!"

2. Say, "I finished the report," or
    "I did all my homework," or
    "I emptied the dishwasher," or

    _____

    (whatever you want acknowledgment for).

3. Receive your applause. If it doesn't happen
    right away, you might have to —

4. Coach your audience. ("That means you're
    supposed to clap.")

Bounce Back!

Receiving It

Receiving the appreciation once you've requested it, really letting it in, is the trickiest part of Ta-DAH. Some of us were taught we shouldn't need it so we hide from it or fend it off. But acknowledgment is actually a very basic human need. I could put all kinds of sociological and psychological footnotes here. But I'm not gonna. You know it's true.

Letting the Audience
Give Something Back

I learned how to receive applause from Lily Tomlin, one of our modern-day comedic masters.

At the end of her awesome performance in *The Search for Intelligent Life in the Universe*, a tidal wave of applause rolled from the audience to the stage. It could have been quite overwhelming, I think, on the receiving end.

Lily Tomlin gathered up the applause and brought it into her heart, spreading her arms out wide to receive, and sweeping them into the center of her chest, then sweeping them back out again to return it to her audience and receive some more. She did this gesture several times. Part of her gift to her audience was allowing us to fully give something back to her.

Bounce Back!

The Full Ta-DAH!

When I was in clown school, my classmates and I practiced doing the tiniest of feats and inviting applause with the most enormous of Ta-DAHs. (I picked up a handkerchief with . . . my TEETH!) It was a wonderfully goofy way to practice having a full transaction with the audience.

Try it.

Draw attention to an accomplishment ("I tied my shoes!"), boldly proclaim Ta-DAH! and receive your applause by bringing it into your heart with your hands.

(Of course, there are subtler ways to ask for and receive appreciation. But subtle is not our business at the moment.)

Giving It to Someone Else

We are constantly surrounded by exhibits of beauty, courage, mastery and kindness, but many of these events go unacknowledged.

You can do something about this!

When you see a natural wonder (an incredible sunset! a co-worker pulling off an amazing project! your child cleaning up a mess without even being asked!), draw attention to it by pointing to it and ringing out an exuberant "Ta-DAH!"

Then lead the applause.

HA!
Laugh for no good reason.

What Are You Waiting For?

There is a common misconception that you have to be coerced into laughter with a joke or some other excuse. Actually, you can start laughing for absolutely no reason at all. At first it may feel fake, but if you stay with it for a minute or two AND KEEP GOING, especially if you are in a group of people, you will find that you are actually REALLY LAUGHING.

People started getting together for this reason in laughing clubs in India, and now in the US and other countries too. But you can start it up informally wherever you are.

THE SECRET: Don't be afraid to look foolish. Just laugh until everyone joins in. Then enjoy the endorphins. This is an absolutely free "high."

It's Your Choice

Song lyrics are on the next page.

Indication: Feelings of fatigue, discouragement, or the blahs.

Application: Hum it, sing it, play it as a drum solo on your desk.

It's Your Choice

Words and Music by Lynn Grasberg

1. Sometimes life is easy and you're right on the money.
   Other times it's hard and it just doesn't seem funny.
   That's the time to step back, take another look,
   Take another tack and just rewrite the Book
   Of Life, of Life, of Life.

   Chorus: It's your choice. (3x)

2. Sometimes you feel like you just can't cope
   And like your world is standing still.
   That's not the time to give up hope.
   The remedy is close at hand if only you will
   Get up and move around.
   Open up your mouth and let out some sound,
   And while you're at it, shake your chakras up and down.
   It's your choice.

   (Chorus)

3. Sometimes you feel like you're just out of touch.
   Chances are that you're not getting touched too much.
   That's the time to reach out and take a chance,
   Take a chance and ask another mammal to dance.
   So take my paw
   And stroke my fur,
   And if you want me to,
   I'll do the same for you.

   (Chorus)

   ©Lynn Grasberg 1990

Part 5

Leading from the Laugh Side of the Brain

Creating Seaworthy Organizations and Individuals

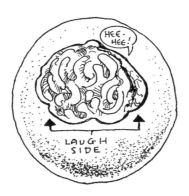

Bounce Back!

Help Wanted

Anyone who can't laugh these days is in BIG TROUBLE. We need to help each other find healthy ways to release the fear, anger and stress of our current situations. And, of course, we need encouragement to let our joy and delight out too.

Wanted: As many laugh leaders as we can get. (They can come from anywhere in an organization.) You are invited to sign up for this venture right now.

....
Sign on the dotted line

Bounce Back!

Re-Define "Work"

Work Ethic: Get the job done no matter how expensive it is to your health, your relationships and your dreams.

Play Ethic: Have fun and get things done. Re-define "work" so it supports your (and others') well-being*.

*Well-being includes, but is not limited to:
- Physical health (feeling rested, calm and energetic).
- The joy of accomplishment.
- Feeling competent and appreciated.
- The ability to relax.
- A sense of connection to oneself and other people.

Learning to Juggle
on the Fly

There are days when the world seems like it's turned upside down. We are thrown into situations where we have to deal with all sorts of changes while simultaneously taking care of everyday needs, carrying out repairs, and inventing new ways to do things as old systems break down. Yikes!

Create a High HQ Environment

We're not talking about making tiny cosmetic changes to the face of business and how we have previously done things.

We're talking about creating a **High HQ** culture designed to handle the unexpected — high and low tides in the economy, hurricane winds, blizzards, droughts . . . and stuff we can't even name because we've never experienced it yet.

In the world of mixed metaphors on the high seas, this is where the rubber meets the road so we can BOUNCE BACK, no matter what.

Put the Play Ethic to Work

Here are a few recommendations for applying **Bounce Back!** principles and techniques from previous chapters in your business.*

Why? So you can think and act more flexibly to meet the demands of rapid change AND BRING YOUR ORGANIZATION WITH YOU!

*If you're between jobs due to downsizing, etc., your current business is finding or creating new work for yourself. This is when you REALLY get to test the principles and techniques for maintaining your sense of humor and well-being.

Recommendations for a High HQ Workplace:

1. Practice *Yes-and* on the job.

2. Embrace diversity.

3, Make the most of mistakes and surprises.

4. Set up a culture of appreciation.

   And while you're at it:

5. Move your body and

6. Laugh out loud.

Practice *Yes-and* on the Job
Maximize Talent.

Be willing to entertain any idea, especially those that shake up "the way we've always done things around here."

Practice *Yes-and* by being open to ideas (from your own brain or others) and see what happens when you expand on them. We humans constantly come up with the most amazing innovations when we're encouraged.

Yes-and in Progress

A: Hey! I've got a great idea.
   [This person is already "yessing" themselves.]
   I think we should . . .

B: Yes, and . . . .

A: Great idea! [another way to say yes]
   AND what if we . . .

C: [Walking into the break room for a snack]
   Yes! And . . .

B: I love that! Why don't we also . . .

A: Yeah! And wouldn't it be a kick if we . . .?

C: Yes, and then we could . . .

B: [Laughing] Do you think we've gone too far?

A: Not yet.

Embrace Diversity

This is a logical extension of **Yes-and.**

Find and support the gifts of each individual in your groups and teams, especially in places where people come from different backgrounds and points of view. Everyone has important pieces of the wisdom and information needed to solve everyday problems and design large-scale changes.

Waddaya Mean by "Diversity?"

I mean the myriad of differences in people.

I'm talking about people from all real and imagined subdivisions of the human race: right and left-brained people, all genders, ethnic and religious groups, rural, urban and suburban folk, middle class, working class and wealthy, straight, gay, old, young, black, yellow, red, white . . . and the diversity within each one of us that cannot be classified.

Life as a Person of Many Colors

I have some experience with prejudice and being perceived as different. When I'm visible as a rainbow clown, I am often judged and discounted (not taken "seriously").

Before they get to know me, people have been known to pre-judge me as too immature, too loud, too shy, too excited, too dangerous, too dumb, too scary, too irresponsible, too embarrassing, too lazy, too erratic, too sloppy, too picky, too happy, too angry, too _____ (fill in the blank). You name it, someone has judged me that way.

Dealing with Ism's (Racism, Ageism, Ablebodyism, Clownism, etc.)

The problem: All kinds of people judge each other in many of the ways noted on the preceding page even though they have little or no actual information about each other.

The solution: Actually get to know individuals instead of seeing people as whatever labels they or other people have hung on them. Make sure everyone (including you) is treated well.

- Be willing to make mistakes while you are getting to know someone.
- Apologize when you do, and don't go away if someone "takes it the wrong way."
- Find things to appreciate and enjoy together.
- Be persistent. Your life gets much richer with a wide variety of close friends and colleagues.

Make the Most of
Mistakes and Surprises

From laughs to new products, take advantage of the gifts in unexpected results . . . and build on them.

Stop hiding mis-takes and start mining them for gold. Some of the best stuff happens when we give up our idea of "what's s'posed to be" and start playing with what is really right in front of us.

Oops in Action

1. My friend made an office call to complete a sale with a new customer but ended up at another similarly named business. ("Oops. 'Scuse me, I was looking for _____.") He ended up getting a BIG order from the "wrong" customer.

2. Lots of inventions started out as "mistakes." Dr. Spence Silver, in search of a strong adhesive in a laboratory at 3M, concocted a material that only stuck temporarily and seemed useless until eventually it was used to make Post-Its™.

Set Up a Culture of Appreciation

Appreciate yourself and other people A LOT. Most people will have to practice to get good at this.

The problem: Most of us were taught that behavior and accomplishments approaching perfection were to be "expected" and anything else needed to be "corrected." We were subjected to lots of criticism and learned to be critical, often most devastatingly, to ourselves.

The solution: Take as many opportunities as possible to go Ta-DAH!, to appreciate yourself and to direct appreciation to others. Practice makes perfect (or at least, very very good).

Ta-DAH!
(Version 1.0)
(Directing Appreciation Toward Oneself)

A: How are things going?

B: I just made 72 corrections on our annual report.

A: Wow! That's great.

B: You're right. Ta-DAH!

Everybody: Wild applause and cheers.

Ta-DAH!
(Version 1.1)
(Directing Appreciation to Someone Else)

A: How are things going?

B: I just made 72 corrections on our annual report.

A: [gesturing toward B]
Ta-DAH!

Everybody: Wild applause and cheers.

Ta-DAH!
(Version 1.2)
(Appreciation Basic Model)

A: How are things going?

B: I just made 72 corrections on our annual report.

A: Thank you. I really appreciate your incredible eye for detail. It's great to be able to count on you to make our documents look so professional.

(This is more of a personal, private Ta-DAH! than versions 1.0 and 1.1, but it is definitely *just as important*.)

And while you're at it . . .

Move Your Body
Don't just sit around.

Traditionally, people accomplish this with trips to the restroom, water cooler and coffee machine (not necessarily in that order).

Expand your repertoire with a variety of ways to move during the day. Your body will feel better and you will think more clearly.

Movement Possibilities

- Stand up and stretch. In different directions.
- Do the Warm-up from p. 96, especially with other people.
- Take a break to go for a walk or a run or
- Jump up and down (especially if you have a mini-trampoline).

Any of these will get your blood moving, make you more alert and improve your mood.

Laugh Out Loud!

Don't just type LOL on your computer screen. Get up and do it!

You have nothing to lose but your stress and your serious self-image.

Take frequent opportunities to be animated and playful, not only on breaks but while working. The best encouragement is modeling this yourself and appreciating others when they dare to do it too.

AND REMEMBER . . .

Your Life Is More Important
Than Your Job.

Jobs and projects come and go. Your life goes on: before, during and after.

You Teach What You Need to Learn
(And, hopefully, eventually, you "get it.")

As I was writing this book, there were several times when I hit lulls in the work. My old training to worry and feel bad about this kicked in until I remembered to APPLY WHAT I WAS WRITING ABOUT (what a concept!).

I made a sign to remind myself of what I needed to remember to finish the book and I coached several friends to tell me these things when I forgot them. (My friends then asked for copies of these messages to post over THEIR desks.)

Warning: These are "radical" messages if you're used to the blame and shame method of motivation.

I have complete
confidence in you
to finish this project
and do a beautiful job.

I care more about
YOU
than the project.

Bounce Back!

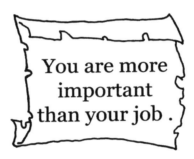

You are more
important
than your job .

Planetary Soup

Song lyrics are on the next page.

Indication: When the newspaper is filled with awful headlines and dire predictions and you need to:

1. Get in touch with the big picture.
2. Renew your hope.
3. Celebrate life and your part in it.

Application: 1. Sing it in your head

or

2. Sing it into an imaginary microphone and broadcast it to the world

or

(for the truly inspired)

3. Accompany yourself on air guitar and other intangible instruments.

Planetary Soup
Words and Music by Lynn Grasberg

Shift happens.
A lot (a lot, a lot, a lot)
Faster and faster
(and faster and faster)
All over the planet.

We're all swimmin'
(swimmin', swimmin', swimmin'),
All the children, all the women,
And every man,
We're all swimmin', swimmin'
As best as we can,
Swimmin' in this Planetary Soup.
We're quite a group.

You can be a laugh leader.
You can laugh out loud and free
Wherever you are
And where you're gonna be,
You can make the first move
To go planetary,
To reach out (reach out, reach out, reach out)
To other people.

I know that you're the best person to do it
And so am I (am I, am I).
I know you knew I knew you knew it,
And here's the (here's the) reason why:
Because we're HERE,
Right now,
Right here,
Right now,
Swimmin' in this Planetary Soup.

Have compassion for yourself
And everybody else.
It's better for your mind
— and your health.
Be bold, be brave,
Make a lot of good mistakes,
And remember (remember, remember, remember)
You've got what it takes
Cuz you're not alone
In your planetary home.

We're all swimmin'
(swimmin', swimmin', swimmin'),
All the children, all the women,
And every man,
We're all swimmin', swimmin'
As best as we can,
Swimmin' in this Planetary Soup.

© Lynn Grasberg 2002

*To order the **Bounce Back!** music CD and*
get a $5 discount plus FREE shipping,
go to www.bounceback.biz/CD.

Bounce Back!

What It Is

It's
an
interesting
unpredictable
smart-ass
universe

And here we are

So that must say something about us

Cuz

We're part of it

Even
if
we
forget
now
and
then.

Bounce Back!

Epilogue

Once upon a time, not so far away and not so far in the future, everyone woke up to the fact that they lived in a state of perpetual change.

And since they could not control this by worrying, they learned to accept and improvise upon the gifts of each moment.

And they all lived boldly ever after.

End Notes

Many thanks to

p. 23   James and Magaly Rodriguez Mossman for the term, "inclusive humor."

p. 49   Charlie Varon who coined the term "Serious Men's Syndrome."

p. 72   Viola Spolin, Paul Sills, Keith Johnstone and all the teachers and improvisers who have taught and modeled *"Yes-and"* throughout the years.

p. 111 Cherie Brown for introducing me to the Welcoming Committee.

p. 124 Madan Kataria for inventing and promoting Laughing Clubs.

Bounce Back!

RESOURCES

Books

Adams, Patch, M.D. with Maureen Mylander. *Gesundheit! Bringing good health to you, the medical system, and society through physician service, complementary therapies, humor, and joy.* Rochester, Vermont: Healing Arts Press. Revised edition, 1998.

Cousins, Norman. *Anatomy of an Illness as Percieved by the Patient.* NY: W.W. Norton & Company. 1979.
_____. *Head First: The Biology of Hope and the Healing Power of the Human Spirit.* NY: Dutton. 1981.

Glickstein, Lee. *Be Heard Now! Tap into Your Inner Speaker and Communicate with Ease.* NY: Broadway Books. 1998.

Goodheart, Annette, Ph.D. *Laughter Therapy: How to Laugh About Everything in Your Life that Isn't Really Funny.* Santa Barbara: Less Stress Press. 1994.

Hilts, Elizabeth. *Getting in Touch with Your Inner Bitch.* Bridgeport, CT: Hysteria Publications. 1994.

Jackins, Harvey. *The Human Side of Human Beings.* Seattle: Rational Island Press. 1974.

Johnstone, Keith. *IMPRO.* NY: Theatre Arts Books. Reprinted 1991.

Levine, Peter A. with Ann Frederick. *Waking the Tiger: Healing Trauma.* Berkeley: North Atlantic Books. 1997.

Nachmanovitch, Stephen. *Free Play: The Power of Improvisation in Life and the Arts.* NY: Jeremy P. Tarcher. 1990.

Oldak, Emily. *Comedy for Real Life: A Guide for Helping Kids Survive in an Imperfect World.* Aurora, CO: The Comedy Prescription. 1999.

Pert, Candace B., Ph.D. *Molecules of Emotion: The Science Behind Mind-Body Medicine.* NY: Simon and Schuster. 1997.

Paulson, Terry. *Making Humor Work: Take Your Job Seriously and Yourself Lightly.* Los Altos, CA; Crisp Publications, 1989.

Rosenberg, Marshall, PhD. *Non-Violent Communication: A Language of Compassion.* Encinitas, CA: PuddleDancer Press. 1999.

Siegal, Bernie, MD. *Love, Medicine and Miracles: Lessons Learned about Self-Healing from a Surgeon's Experience with Exceptional Patients.* NY: HarperCollins. 1986.

Spolin, Viola. *Improvisation for the Theater.* Evanston, IL: Northwestern University Press. 1963.

Varon, Charlie. *Rush Limbaugh in Night School.* NY: Dramatists Play Service. 1997. Other plays: *Ralph Nader is Missing, The People's Violin.*

CDs

Grasberg, Lynn. ***Bounce Back!***
Pagosa Springs: Morningstar Communications LLC. 2002.
Songs and other surprises. Companion CD to this book.
(877) 587-4872   www.bounceback.biz

Rhiannon. *flight: Rhiannon's Interactive Guide to Vocal Improvisation.*
Boulder: Sounds True, 2000. (800) 333-9185. www.soundstrue.com
Very encouraging and inspiring. Will help you open your voice and find creativity you didn't know you had.

McFerrin, Bobby, ANY of his stuff. He brings the spirit of improvisation to all his music.

Websites

www.bounceback.biz
• Bring Lynn Grasberg and her ***Bounce Back!*** programs to your meeting, conference or corporate retreat.
• Raise your HQ with ***Bounce Back!*** song sheets, articles, books, CDs, and humor supplements.

www.larrywilde.com
From the originator of National Humor Month (30 days for April Fools). Tune in here for another take on the health benefits of laughter.

www.rc.org
Re-Evaluation Counseling. Excellent organization for learning how to exchange counseling with peers to uncover your full intelligence and other human qualities (including humor, of course).

About the Author

 **Lynn Grasberg,** aka Penelope the Clown, was born on April Fool's Day, is the former director of the San Francisco School of ReMirthing and is currently Chief Comic Officer for Humor Relations Associates. As a keynote speaker, corporate trainer and presentation coach, she helps her clients use humor to handle serious issues.

Lynn's long list of laughing clients includes American Medical Response, Copic Insurance Company, Denver Public Library, Dominican College, HUD, Int'l Association of Facilitators, Lawrence Livermore Labs, Lucent Technologies, Marketing and Advertising Council, Merrill Lynch Realty, Mizel Museum, Storage Tek, Tagawa Inc., UC Medical Center, US West (Qwest) and Qualife.

Lynn also lights up the stage as a professional actress and musical comedienne. One of her most challenging roles (she learned to play the bagpipe for it!) was Willie the Piper in *Tokens*, a musical produced in San Francisco by Whoopi Goldberg.

Lynn's audiences at festivals and conferences have included Women in Leadership at Lucent; Vancouver Folk Festival (with Patch Adams); Diversity Associates International; AIDS, Medicine and Miracles; Boulder Jewish Festival; AEE, BVSD, CWA, EE/OA, IAF, PTSD and lots of other alphabet soups, where she brings people together through a shared sense of humor and play.

Lynn Grasberg/*Bounce Back!*
P. O. Box 4116
Pagosa Springs, CO 81157
877-587-4872

Index

Visit Lynn Grasberg's website at
www.bounceback.biz

Share stories with other readers about your experiences with the ideas and practices from this book.

Sign up for our monthly e-zine.

Find out how to bring Lynn Grasberg and her **Bounce Back!** programs to your meeting, conference or corporate retreat.

Raise your HQ with **Bounce Back!** song sheets, articles, books, CDs and humor supplements.

Get a $5 discount plus FREE shipping on the **Bounce Back!** music CD, go to www.bounceback.biz/CD.

Ta-DAH!

Bounce Back!